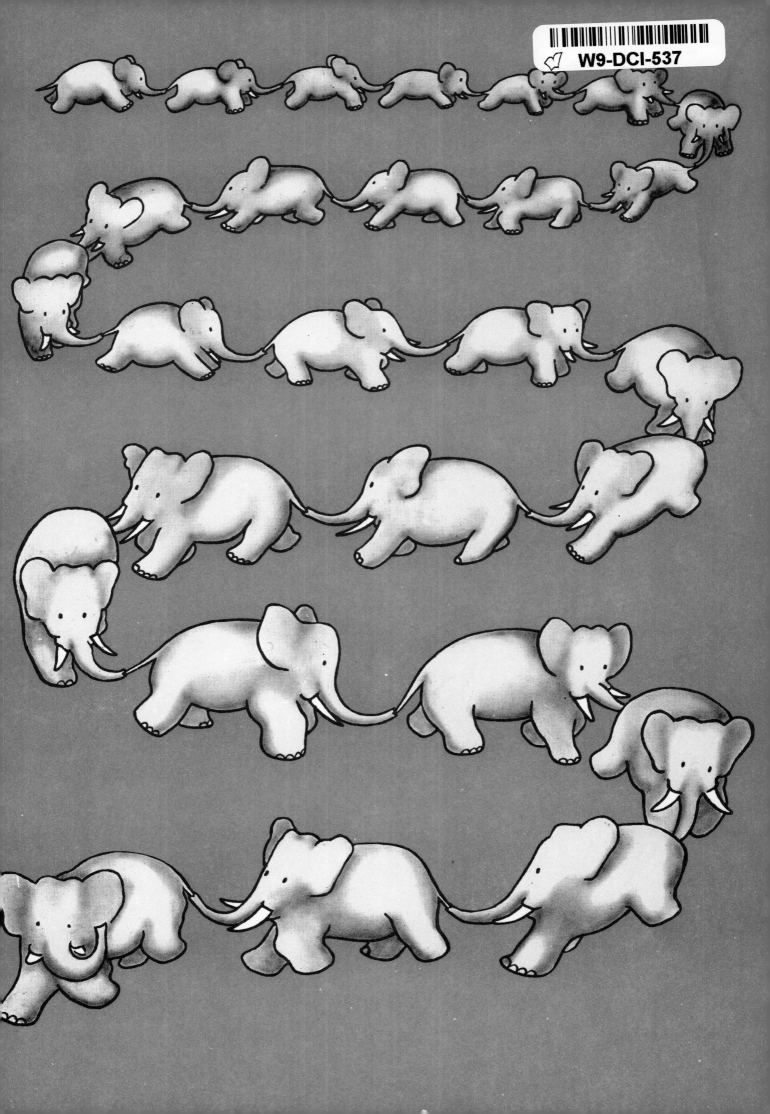

The lovable little elephant who has endeared himself to children all over the world for more than a quarter of a century now gives his young American friends some Spanish lessons.

And how delightful they are! Babar knows what boys and girls like, and so he has chosen to instruct them in those words and phrases that they are most likely to use from day to day.

To make the lessons easier, the Spanish words are printed in red, while the English translations of those words stand out in bold-face type.

LAURENT DE BRUNHOFF

BABAR'S

SPANISH LESSONS

LAS LECCIONES ESPAÑOLES DE

BABAR

Spanish words by Roberto Eyzaguirre

RANDOM HOUSE   New York

© Copyright, 1965, 1963, by Random House, Inc.

1 YO SOY BABAR, EL REY DE LOS ELEFANTES

I am Babar, king of the elephants. Last summer during my vacation in Spain I learned Spanish. Would you like me to teach you some Spanish? Very well. Soon you will be able to make yourself understood in countries where the language is spoken.

The picture shows you how I look. Now say with me:

My head is mi cabeza.

My ears are mis orejas.

My nose is mi nariz. I mean **my trunk** is mi trompa.

And **my eyes** are mis ojos.

Now you must learn what I wear. Isn't that a wonderful suit of a becoming color?

This is **my green suit,** mi traje verde.

It is **my favorite,** mi favorito.

You say **coat and trousers?** I say chaqueta y pantalón.

I wear **a nice tie**—una bonita corbata—with **a pink shirt,** una camisa rosada.

What else? **My crown and my shoes.** Mi corona y mis zapatos.

That is enough for the first lesson!

2 TODAS LAS MAÑANAS ME DUCHO

Every morning I take a shower. First **a cold shower**—una ducha fría—because I remain sleepy otherwise.

Then **a warm shower**—una ducha caliente.

I wash myself. Yo me lavo.

My skin is thick, so I have to use a big brush with the soap. **A brush** is un cepillo. **Soap** is jabón.

I rub my arms. Me froto los brazos.

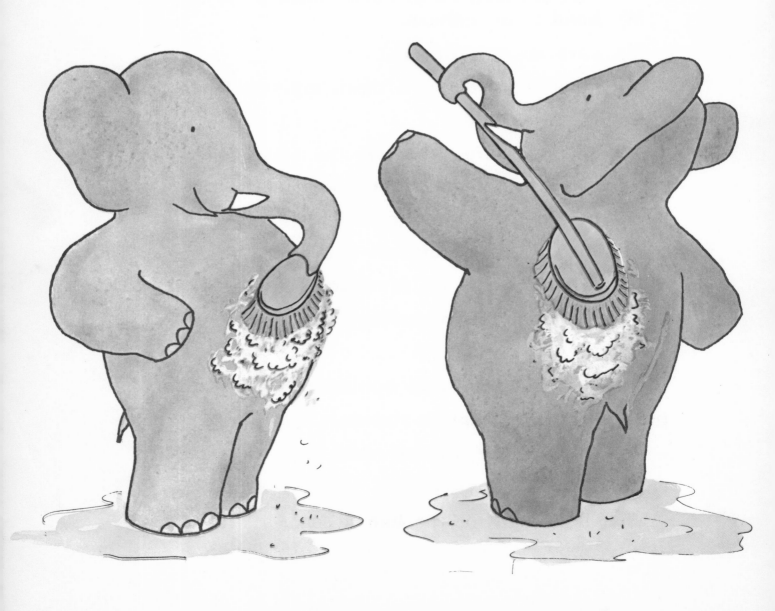

I **rub my stomach.** Me froto el vientre.

I **rub my back.** Me froto la espalda.

I **rub my left leg.** Me froto la pierna iz-
quierda.

I **rub my right leg.** Me froto la pierna
derecha.

And while I rub myself, **I sing.** Canto. Do
you sing when you are under the shower? What
you certainly don't do is to shower yourself with
a trunk. Only elephants can do that!

Then I take **a large towel**—una toalla grande
—and **I dry myself.** Me seco.

And **I put on my clothes.** Me pongo la ropa.

Then I am ready. Ya estoy listo.

And this is enough for your second lesson.

3   EL DESAYUNO ES DELICIOSO

Breakfast is delicious.

What do you like **to eat**—comer—for breakfast?

I like to eat cereal, but my wife, Queen Celeste, prefers **a slice of bread and butter**—una rebanada de pan con mantequilla—or **a slice of toast**—un pan tostado.

We drink a cup of tea. Tomamos una taza de té. Here are **my children**—mis hijos: Pom, Flora, Alexander and Cousin Arthur.

"Good morning, Daddy," they say. "Buenos días, Papá."

The children drink **hot chocolate**—chocolate caliente. They all love **crescents**—medias lunas. What are

these? Delicious rolls. The French bakers are noted for them, but you can find them in Spain also.

Arthur is greedy. Arturo es goloso. He puts **four pieces of sugar**—cuatro terrones de azúcar—in his chocolate. Then he mixes it carefully with **a spoon**—una cucharita.

Pom is always hungry. Pom siempre tiene hambre. When the crescents are all eaten, he asks for bread. He puts a lot of butter on it with **a knife**—un cuchillo—and he adds **jam**—conserva—or **honey**—miel.

These are quite a few words for a third lesson, but breakfast is very important, **isn't it?** No es verdad?

4 LOS NIÑOS VAN A LA ESCUELA

The children are going to school.

One, two, three, four, five. Uno, dos, tres, cuatro, cinco. There are five children going to school.

Five pupils—cinco alumnos—who meet five others: six, seven, eight, nine, ten. Seis, siete, ocho, nueve, diez.

There are ten pupils carrying ten briefcases—diez cartapacios—on the way to school.

The Old Lady, the teacher—la Maestra—is a very good friend of mine. Her pupils love her very much.

"Well, children," she says, "pick up your notebooks—vuestros cuadernos—and your pens—vuestras plumas.

"Be careful not to make **ink spots**—manchas de tinta. Ready? Copy down what **I read**—leo: 'The rabbit eats carrots and . . .'

"Now children, **open your books**—abrid vuestros libros—to page 27, **please**—por favor. Compare it with what you have written. Then take

your pencils—vuestros lápices—and correct **your mistakes**—vuestras faltas."

After that, **she writes on the blackboard**—ella escribe en la pizarra—with **a piece of chalk**—un pedazo de tiza.

I like to go for a walk in the garden. There are **flowers of all colors**—flores de todos los colores.

Red	**Yellow**	**Blue**	**Pink**
Rojo	Amarillo	Azul	Rosado

Celeste comes along and gathers flowers to make **a bouquet**—un ramo. She loves **the roses**—las rosas. (See, it is almost the same word in English and Spanish.)

Really, this is not a difficult lesson, is it?

But now let's see which **tools**—herramientas—I need for working in the garden.

With **a rake**—un rastrillo—I clean **the path**—el andador. Into **the wheelbarrow**—la carretilla—I put **the leaves**—las hojas—which have fallen from **the trees**—los árboles.

I have **vegetables**—legumbres—and **fruits**—frutas. (Another word that is almost the same in both languages!)

See **the scarecrow**—el espantajo? It frightens away **the birds**—los pájaros—that might eat the fruit and vegetables.

I myself made the scarecrow with a very old suit and a hat that Celeste did not want me to wear any more.

6 MI CASA TIENE TRES PISOS

My house has three floors.

From **the balcony of my room**—el balcón de mi cuarto—I can see **the roofs**—los techos—of Celesteville down to the lake.

Most of the time I stay in **the library**—la biblioteca. It is a quiet room and I like to leave **the window open**—la ventana abierta. All **the walls**—las paredes—are lined with **books**—libros.

When I read, I sit in **an armchair**—un sillón. When I write I use **the chair**—la silla—at **the table**—la mesa.

Every day after school, the children knock at **the door**—la puerta. I say, **"Come in." "Adelante."** Then the three of them rush in to kiss me. Flora goes to the balcony, Alexander sits down on **the rug**—la alfombra—and Pom asks me what I'm doing.

Sometimes I still have to work at night, when my children are asleep (when you too are asleep), because being a king is a hard job. Then I like **the curtains closed**—las cortinas cerradas—and **a fire**—el fuego—burning **in the chimney**—en la chimenea francesa. And **I light my pipe**—enciendo mi pipa.

7 LA COCINERA ESTÁ COCINANDO

The Old Lady is cooking.

She is going to make **a chocolate cake**—una torta de chocolate—the children's favorite.

On the kitchen table—sobre la mesa de la cocina—she puts these things:

½ pound chocolate	2 tablespoons of rice flour instead of
¼ pound sugar	**flour**—harina
¼ pound butter	¼ pound of **shredded almonds**—
6 **eggs**—6 huevos	almendras picadas

While the Old Lady softens the chocolate, Celeste softens the butter and Flora carefully beats **the whites of the eggs**—las claras de los huevos—very stiff. The Old Lady mixes everything in **a big bowl**—una gran fuente. Then she puts **the dough**—la masa—in a rather flat **baking pan**—tortera. She must leave it **in the oven**—en el horno—at a low heat for about 45 minutes.

But Pom can hardly wait. He gets **his plate and his fork**—su plato y su tenedor. He wants to be all prepared **to taste**—para probar—the delicious cake.

You may try **the recipe**—la receta—but do not eat **too large a piece**—un pedazo demasiado grande.

I play with the children.

They like **to play soccer**—jugar al fútbol.

Yes, I mean "football" because your game of soccer is what we call football and your game of football is what we call Rugby.

Isn't that funny?

Arthur likes to be **the goal-keeper**—el portero.

"Pom, **pass the ball!**"—"pásame la pelota!" shouts Alexander.

But Pom won't pass. **He runs**—él corre—and keeps the ball for himself. He kicks . . .

Arthur catches the ball. Arturo coge la pelota. Good for you, Arthur!

But Alexander teasingly says: "Oh, Pom, you are so **clumsy**—torpe. **Look at me.** Mírame." **He kicks the ball.** El da un puntapié a la pelota. The ball rolls out of bounds.

"Missed!" "Erraste!" "Ha! Ha! Ha!" and Pom laughs.

You see, it is amusing to play soccer. In Europe we are as fond of soccer as you are of football or baseball.

But let me ask you something. Who will teach me how to play baseball? We don't have baseball in Europe.

The bicycle ride.

Who wants to go for a bicycle ride **this afternoon**—esta tarde?

Hurray! Bravo! We all want to go. And **right away**—en seguida—we get ready.

"I'll inflate **the tires**—las llantas," says Arthur.

"I'll fix **the brakes**—los frenos," says Zéphir.

"I'll put **a drop of oil on the chain**—una gota de aceite en la cadena," says Pom.

"I'll make a shiny **handlebar**—guía," says Alexander.

"I'll prepare the things for **the picnic**—la jira campestre," says Flora. What excitement!

Then we hop on to **the saddle**—el sillín—and **we pedal**—pedaleamos.

Pom and Alexander race. Pom y Alejandro compiten en una carrera.

"Let me go first!" shouts Alexander. But **he skids**—se resbala—**and falls down**—y se cae.

Poor Alexander! **He cries.** Llora, even though only his pants **are torn**—están desgarrados.

"Cheer up, Alexander," says Zéphir. **"Let's stop here**—paremos aquí—and start on the sandwiches."

Happy Birthday. Today, **April twelfth**—el doce de abril—is **a great day**—un gran día—for the Babars. It is Pom's birthday, and Flora's birthday, and Alexander's, because the three of them were born on the very same day.

They have invited all their friends. Han invitado a todos sus amigos. Celeste has prepared **ice cream**—helados—**cookies**—bizcochitos—**candy and lollipops**—confites y caramelos en palito, lots of **pineapple juice**—jugo de ananás, and a soft drink the children like very much: pink elephant punch.

Pom, Flora and Alexander were so happy with **their presents**—sus regalos—that they kept on their new costumes. Pom feels very daring in his cowboy suit. "Nobody can beat me with **a gun**—una pistola," he says to his admiring friend Catherine.

Flora has received exactly what she wished for: **a nurse's uniform**—un uniforme de enfermera. As for Alexander, he is already telling of his adventures as a space elephant. Later on, Celeste organizes **games**—juegos—and Pom's red cowboy **handkerchief**—pañuelo—is very useful for playing **Blindman's Buff**—la gallina ciega.

My car is fast.

It is a good car with nice lines and a strong **motor**–motor. We like it very much and Flora gave it a name—Josephine.

I need a car with **plenty of room**–muy espacioso–because when I go riding I like to take along the whole family, as well as the Old Lady and Zéphir. That's a lot of people, and only two of them are thin . . .

Today we are going **on vacation**–en vacaciones.

Arthur has helped me to put **the luggage in the trunk**–el equipaje en el baúl. I push **the**

starter—el arranque—and the motor roars. Arthur reminds me to stop at the service station to get **some gas**—gasolina.

The man washes **the windshield**—el parabrisas. Then off we go . . .

I drive—manejo—slowly while we're still **in town**—en la ciudad. But as soon as we're away from the crowds and **the highway is straight and empty**—la carretera es derecha y está vacía—Alexander shouts, **"Faster! Más rápido! Go at full speed!**—a toda velocidad!" And I drive a little faster.

We are going to the seashore.

We are going to swim and to dive.
Vamos a nadar y a zambullirnos. **There
is the beach.** Allí está la playa.

Pom, Flora and Alexander run **on the
sand**—en la arena. They rush **into the
waves**—en las olas. Hop!

Arthur has a spear and **goes fishing**—va
a pescar. He disappears for hours **in the
water**—en el agua.

Have you ever gone swimming wearing
goggles so you could see **the fish and the
rocks**—los peces y las rocas—underwater?

Zéphir prefers **to dig a hole**—hacer un hueco—in
the sand. Where is he? He is hiding in the hole!

The three little ones are making **a castle**—un cas-
tillo. They hope it will stand even when **the tide**—la
marea—comes in. Flora decorates the castle with **shells
and little pebbles**—conchas y pequeños guijarros.

She is a real artist!

The Old Lady likes to rest under **the beach umbrella**—el parasol.

And I go out with Celeste in **my sailboat**—mi barco
de vela.

This is the best vacation in the world.

Good weather and bad weather.

Yesterday—ayer—was a fine day and we could say: **"The sun is shining. Brilla el sol."** Yesterday we needed **sunglasses**—anteojos ahumados —and **straw hats**—sombreros de paja.

But **today it is raining**—hoy está lloviendo. I hope **the rain**—la lluvia—will stop **tomorrow**—mañana. We can see **the drops**—las gotas—dripping down on the window pane. Drip, drip, drip!

It is impossible **to go out**—salir—without **an umbrella**—un paraguas—or a rain hat and raincoat and **boots**—chanclos. Tell me, when you see **puddles**—charcos—do you like to jump into them? That's not very nice. But Alexander does it and Flora cries when she is splashed with **mud**—lodo.

I don't like rain, but I love **snow**—la nieve.

It is such fun to throw **snowballs**—bolas de nieve—to build **a snow man**—un muñeco de nieve, and **to go skiing**—ir a esquiar. Or just stare at **the snowflakes**—los copos de nieve.

My bed is comfortable.

When **I am tired**—estoy fatigado—at the end of the day it is good **to go to bed**—acostarse.

I take off **my robe**—mi bata—and **my slippers**—mis pantuflas—and make sure I have **a glass of water**—un vaso de agua—near me.

I pull **the blanket**—la frazada—up to my neck.

Usually **I fall asleep very quickly**—me duermo muy rápidamente.

Do you have **nice dreams**—sueños agradables? I do. But sometimes I have **nightmares**—pesadillas. Then **I wake up suddenly**—me despierto bruscamente.

Now, my friends, **I am very sleepy**—tengo mucho sueño. I **turn out the light**—apago la luz.

Good night. Buenas noches. And **thank you**—gracias—for having learned your Spanish lessons so well.

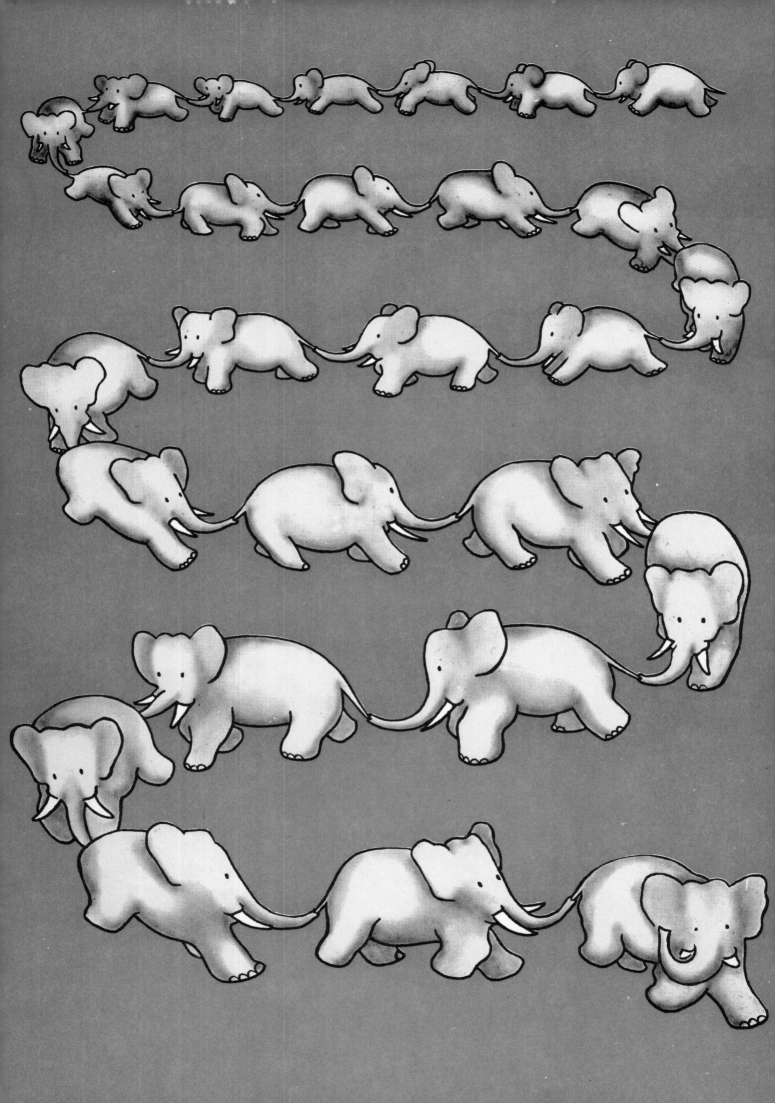